D1798469

The Poetry Of Katherine Tynan – Volume 1

Katherine Tynan was born on January 23rd 1859 into a large farming family in Clondalkin, County Dublin, and educated at a convent school in Drogheda. In her early years she suffered from eye ulcers, which left her somewhat myopic.

She first began to have her poems published in 1878. A great friend to Gerard Manley Hopkins and to WB Yeats (who it is rumoured proposed marriage but was rejected). With Yeats to encourage her, her poetry blossomed and she was equally supportive of his. She married fellow writer and barrister Henry Albert Hinkson in 1898. They moved to England where she bore and began to raise 5 children although two were to tragically die in infancy. In 1912 they returned to Claremorris, County Mayo when her husband was appointed magistrate there from 1912 until 1919. Sadly her husband died that year but Katherine continued to write.

Her output was prolific, some sources have her as the author of almost a 100 novels. Here we concentrate on her poetry. Amongst the classics such as 'The Wind That Shakes The Barley' are numerous war poems. She is now sometimes grouped amongst the War Poets of the First World War. Her experience was not direct but as a Mother with one son serving in France and another in Palestine, the emotions, fears and doubts are expressed in a beautiful heart-felt way.

Katherine died on April 2nd 1931 and she is buried at Kensal Green Cemetery in London.

Index Of Poems

The Predestined
To One In Grief

The Wind That Shakes The Barley

There's music in my heart all day,
I hear it late and early,
It comes from fields are far away,
The wind that shakes the barley.

Above the uplands drenched with dew
The sky hangs soft and pearly,
An emerald world is listening to
The wind that shakes the barley.

Above the bluest mountain crest
The lark is singing rarely,
It rocks the singer into rest,
The wind that shakes the barley.

Oh, still through summers and through springs
It calls me late and early.
Come home, come home, come home, it sings,
The wind that shakes the barley.

Sheep And Lambs

All in the April evening,
April airs were abroad;
The sheep with their little lambs
Passed me by on the road.

The sheep with their little lambs
Passed me by on the road;
All in the April evening
I thought on the Lamb of God.

The lambs were weary and crying
With a weak, human cry.
I thought on the Lamb of God
Going meekly to die.

Up in the blue, blue mountains
Dewy pastures are sweet;
Rest for the little bodies,
Rest for the little feet.

But for the Lamb of God,
Up on the hill-top green,
Only a Cross of shame

Two stark crosses between.

All in the April evening,
April airs were abroad;
I saw the sheep with their lambs,
And thought on the Lamb of God.

Mater Dei
She looked to east, she looked to west,
Her eyes, unfathomable, mild,
That saw both worlds, came home to rest,
Home to her own sweet child.
God's golden head was at her breast.

What need to look o'er land and sea?
What could the winged ships bring to her?
What gold or gems of price might be,
Ivory or miniver,
Since God Himself lay on her knee?

What could th' intense blue heaven keep
To draw her eyes and thoughts so high?
All heaven was where her Boy did leap,
Where her foot quietly
Went rocking the dear God asleep.

The angel folk fared up and down
A Jacob's Ladder hung between

Her quiet chamber and God's Town.
She saw unawed, serene;
Since God Himself played by her gown.

When You Come Home
All will be right when you come home, dear lad,
But oh, 'tis long of coming that you are!
Everything's wrong with all the world and sad;
There are so many hurt in this long war,
So many missing, who will never come,
Lying out in the rain and in the cold.
I shall forget it all when you come home,
I shall forget the lonesome things they told.

There's something, something sad, that troubles me.
Beats like the rain upon my frightened heart;
A tale about a girl, the thing might be,
Whispered in corners, secret and apart
How he was killed and how she never knew
Because God put a small cloud on her mind,

And how she waited the black winters through
And the wet summers; surely God was kind!

I took a daisy from the garden-bed
And plucked the petals, one by one, to tell
When I and my true lover should be wed,
This year: Next year: Never: the petals fell
And stopped at Never. But it could not guess,
The foolish daisy, what true love I had.
I turned from daisies and I plucked heartsease
To rest my heart on and be safe and glad.

Everything's wrong, Love, since you went away,
Such a queer world when all the boys are gone,
And there is no one left but old and grey,
Women and children, frightened and alone.
Sometimes the tale is crying at my heart
Of that poor girl. Maybe 'twas but a dream.
When you come home the shadows will depart,
The lonesome dreams die off in morning gleam.

Lambs
He sleeps as a lamb sleeps,
Beside his mother.
Somewhere in yon blue deeps
His tender brother
Sleeps like a lamb and leaps.

He feeds as a lamb might,
Beside his mother.
Somewhere in fields of light
A lamb, his brother,
Feeds, and is clothed in white.

Old Song Re-Sung
I saw three ships a-sailing,
A-sailing on the sea,
The first her masts were silver,
Her hull was ivory.
The snows came drifting softly,
And lined her white as wool;
Oh, Jesus, Son of Mary,
Thy Cradle beautiful!

I saw three ships a-sailing,
The next was red as blood,
Her decks shone like a ruby,
Encrimsoned all her wood.
Her main-mast stood up lonely,

A lonely Cross and stark.
Oh, Jesus, Son of Mary,
Bring all men to that ark!

I saw three ships a-sailing.
The third for cargo bore
The souls of men redeemed,
That shall be slaves no more.
The lost beloved faces,
I saw them glad and free.
Oh, Jesus, Son of Mary,
When wilt thou come for me?

Easter
Bring flowers to strew His way,
Yea, sing, make holiday;
Bid young lambs leap,
And earth laugh after sleep.

For now He cometh forth
Winter flies to the north,
Folds wings and cries
Amid the bergs and ice.

Yea, Death, great Death is dead,
And Life reigns in his stead;
Cometh the Athlete
New from dead Death's defeat.

Cometh the Wrestler,
But Death he makes no stir,
Utterly spent and done,
And all his kingdom gone.

The Weeping Babe
She kneels by the cradle
Where Jesus doth lie;
Singing, Lullaby, my Baby!
But why dost Thou cry?

The babes of the village
Smile sweetly in sleep;
And lullaby, my Baby,
That ever dost weep!

I've wrapped Thee in linen,
The gift of the Kings;
And wool, soft and fleecy,
The kind Shepherd brings.

Now smile, little Jesus,
Whom naught can defile;
All gifts will I give Thee
An thou wilt but smile.

But it's lullaby, my Baby!
And mournful am I,
Thou cherished little Jesus,
That still Thou wilt cry.

'Adveniat Regnum Tuum'
Thy kingdom come ! Yea, bid it come!
But when Thy kingdom first began
On earth, Thy kingdom was a home,
A child, a woman, and a man.

The child was in the midst thereof,
O, blessed Jesus, holiest One!
The centre and the fount of love
Mary and Joseph's little Son.

Wherever on the earth shall be
A child, a woman, and a man,
Imaging that sweet trinity
Wherewith Thy kingdom first began,

Establish there Thy kingdom! Yea,
And o'er that trinity of love
Send down, as in Thy appointed day,
The brooding spirit of Thy Dove!

The Legend Of St Austin And The Child
St. Austin, going in thought
Along the sea-sands gray,
Into another world was caught,
And Carthage far away.

He saw the City of God
Hang in the saffron sky;
And this was holy ground he trod,
Where mortals come not nigh.

He saw pale spires aglow,
Houses of heavenly sheen;
All in a world of rose and snow,
A sea of gold and green.
There amid Paradise
The saint was rapt away

From unillumined sands and skies
And floor of muddy clay.

His soul took wings and flew,
Forgetting mortal stain,
Upon the track of that bright crew
That homed to heaven again.

Forgetting mortal dearth
It seized on heavenly things,
Till it was cast again to earth,
Because it had not wings.

Because the Three in One
He could not understand,
Baffled and beaten and undone,
He gazed o'er sea and land.

Then by a little pool
A lovely child he saw;
A harmless thing and beautiful,
And yet so full of awe,

That with a curved sea-shell,
Held in his rosy hand,
Had scooped himself a little well
Within the yielding sand.

And to and fro went he,
Between it and the wave,
Bearing his shell filled with the sea
To find a sandy grave.

'What is it that you do,
You lovely boy and bold?'
'I empty out the ocean blue,
You man so wise and old!

'See you how in this cup
I bind the great sea's girth!'
'Ah no, the gray sands suck it up
Your cup is little worth.

'Now put your play aside,
And let the ocean be.
Tell me your name, O violet-eyed,
That empty out the sea!

'What lineage high and fine
Is yours, O kingly boy,
That sure art sprung of royal line,

A people's hope and joy.'

'Austin, as you have said,
A crown my Sire doth wear,
My mother was a royal maid
And yet went cold and bare.'

He shook his golden curls,
A scornful laugh laughed he:
'The night that I was born, the churls,
They would not shelter me.

'Only the ox and ass,
The night that I was born,
Made me a cradle of the grass
And watched by me till morn.

'The night that I was born
The ass and ox alone,
Betwixt the midnight and the morn,
Knelt down upon the stone.

'The bitter night I came,
Each star sang in its sphere.
Now riddle, riddle me my name,
My Austin, tried and dear.'

Austin is on his face,
Before that vision bright.
'My Lord, what dost Thou in this place
With such a sinful wight?'

'I come not here in wrath,
But I come here in love,
My Austin, skilled in life and death,
Thy vanity to prove.

'Mortal, yet over-bold
To fly where th' eagle flies,
As soon this cup the sea will hold
As thou My Mysteries.

'Patience a little yet,
And thou shalt be with Me,
And in thy soul's small cup unmeet
Myself will pour the sea.'

When Austin raised his head
No child was there beside,
But in the cup the Child had made
There swelled the rising tide.

The End Of The Day

The night darkens fast & the shadows darken,
Clouds & the rain gather about mine house,
Only the wood-dove moans, hearken, O hearken!
The moan of the wood-dove in the rain-wet boughs.

Loneliness & the night! The night is lonely
Star-covered the night takes to a tender breast
Wrapping them in her veil these dark hours only
The weary, the bereaved, the dispossessed.

When will it lighten? Once the night was kindly
Nor all her hours went by leaden & long.
Now in mine house the hours go groping blindly.
After the shiver of dawn, the first bird's song.

Sleep now! The night with wings of splendour swept
Hides heavy eyes from light that they may sleep
Soft & secure, under her gaze so tender
Lest they should wake to weep, should wake to weep.

Immortality

So I have sunk my roots in earth
Since that my pretty boys had birth;
And fear no more the grave and gloom,
I, with the centuries to come.

As the tree blossoms so bloom I,
Flinging wild branches to the sky;
Renew each year my leafy suit,
Strike with the years a deeper root.

Shelter a thousand birds to be,
A thousand herds give praise to me;
And in my kind and grateful shade
How many a weary head be laid.

I clothe myself without a stain.
In me a child is born again,
A child that looks with innocent eyes
On a new world with glad surprise.

The old mistakes are all undone,
All the old sins are purged and gone.
Old wounds and scars have left no trace,
There are no lines in this young face.

To hear the cuckoo the first time,

And 'mid new roses in the prime
To read the poets newly. This,
Year after year, shall be my bliss.

Of me shall love be born anew;
I shall be loved and lover too;
Years after th s poor body has died
Shall be the bridegroom and the bride.

Of me shall mothers spring to know
The mother's bliss, the mother's woe;
And children's children yet to be
Shall learn their prayers about my knee.

And many million lights of home
Shall light for me the time to come.
Unto me much shall be forgiven,
I that make many souls for heaven.

The Only Child
Lest he miss other children, lo!
His angel is his playfellow.
A riotous angel two years old,
With wings of rose and curls of gold.

There on the nursery floor together
They play when it is rainy weather,
Building brick castles with much pain,
Only to knock them down again.

Two golden heads together look
An hour long o'er a picture-book,
Or, tired of being good and still,
They play at horses with good will.

And when the boy laughs you shall hear
Another laughter silver-clear,
Sweeter than music of the skies,
Or harps, or birds of Paradise.

Two golden heads one pillow press,
Two rosebuds shut for heaviness.
The wings of one are round the other
Lest chill befall his tender brother.

All day, with forethought mild and grave,
The little angel's quick to save.
And still outruns with tender haste
The adventurous feet that go too fast.

From draughts, from fire, from cold and stings
Wraps him within his gauzy wings;
And knows his father's pride, and shares
His happy mother's tears and prayers.

The Nurse
Such innocent companionship
Is hers, whether she wake or sleep,
'Tis scarcely strange her face should wear
The young child's grave and innocent air.

All the night long she hath by her
The quiet breathing, the soft stir,
Nor knows how in that tender place
The children's angels veil the face.

She wakes at dawn with bird and child
To earth new-washed and reconciled,
The hour of silence and of dew,
When God hath made His world anew.

She sleeps at eve, about the hour
Of bedtime for the bird and flower,
When daisies, evening primroses,
Know that the hour of closing is.

Her daylight thoughts are all on toys
And games for darling girls and boys,
Lest they should fret, lest they should weep,
Strayed from their heavenly fellowship.

She is as pretty and as brown
As the wood's children far from town,
As bright-eyed, glancing, shy of men,
As any squirrel, any wren.

Tender she is to beast and bird,
As in her breast some memory stirred
Of days when those were kin of hers
Who go in feathers and in furs.

A child, yet is the children's law,
And rules by love and rules by awe.
And, stern at times, is kind withal
As a girl-baby with her doll.

Outside the nursery door there lies
The world with all its griefs and sighs,
Its needs, its sins, its stains of sense:
Within is only innocence.

Of St. Francis And The Ass

Our father, ere he went
Out with his brother, Death,
Smiling and well-content
As a bridegroom goeth,
Sweetly forgiveness prayed
From man or beast whom he
Had ever injured
Or burdened needlessly.

'Verily,' then said he,
'I crave before I pass
Forgiveness full and free
Of my little brother, the ass.
Many a time and oft,
When winds and ways were hot,
He hath borne me cool and soft
And service grudged me not.

'And once did it betide
There was, unseen of me,
A gall upon his side
That suffered grievously.
And once his manger was
Empty and bare, and brown.
(Praise God for sweet, dry grass
That Bethlehem folk shook down!)

'Consider, brethern,' said he,
'Our little brother; how mild,
How patient, he will be,
Though men are fierce and wild.
His coat is gray and fine,
His eyes are kind with love;
This little brother of mine
Is gentle as the dove.

'Consider how such an one
Beheld our Saviour born,
And carried him, full-grown,
Through Eastern streets one morn.
For this the Cross is laid
Upon him for a sign.
Greatly is honourèd
This little brother of mine.'

And even while he spake,
Down in his stable stall
His little ass 'gan shake

And turned its face to the wall.
Down fell the heavy tear;
Its gaze so mournful was,
Fra Leo, standing near,
Pitied the little ass.

That night our father died,
All night the kine did low:
The ass went heavy-eyed,
With patient tears and slow.
The very birds on wings
Made mournful cries in the air.
Amen! all living things
Our father's brethern were.

St Francis To The Birds
Little sisters, the birds:
We must praise God, you and I
You, with songs that fill the sky,
I, with halting words.

All things tell His praise,
Woods and waters thereof sing,
Summer, Winter, Autumn, Spring,
And the night and days.

Yea, and cold and heat,
And the sun and stars and moon,
Sea with her monotonous tune,
Rain and hail and sleet,

And the winds of heaven,
And the solemn hills of blue,
And the brown earth and the dew,
And the thunder even,

And the flowers' sweet breath.
All things make one glorious voice;
Life with fleeting pains and joys,
And our brother, Death.

Little flowers of air,
With your feathers soft and sleek,
And your bright brown eyes and meek,
He hath made you fair.

He hath taught to you
Skill to weave in tree and thatch
Nests where happy mothers hatch
Speckled eggs of blue.

And hath children given:
When the soft heads overbrim
The brown nests, then thank ye Him
In the clouds of heaven.

Also in your lives
Live His laws Who loveth you.
Husbands, be ye kind and true;
Be home-keeping, wives:

Love not gossiping;
Stay at home and keep the nest;
Fly not here and there in quest
Of the newest thing.

Live as brethren live:
Love be in each heart and mouth;
Be not envious, be not wroth,
Be not slow to give.

When ye build the nest,
Quarrel not o'er straw or wool;
He who hath be bountiful
To the neediest.

Be not puffed nor vain
Of your beauty or your worth,
Of your children or your birth,
Or the praise ye gain.

Eat not greedily:
Sometimes for sweet mercy's sake,
Worm or insect spare to take;
Let it crawl or fly.

See ye sing not near
To our church on holy day,
Lest the human-folk should stray
From their prayers to hear.

Now depart in peace:
In God's name I bless each one;
May your days be long i' the sun
And your joys increase.

And remember me,
Your poor brother Francis, who
Loves you and gives thanks to you
For this courtesy.

Sometimes when ye sing,
Name my name, that He may take
Pity for the dear song's sake
On my shortcoming.

The Children Of The Lir
Out upon the sand-dunes thrive the coarse long grasses;
Herons standing knee-deep in the brackish pool;
Overhead the sunset fire and flame amasses
And the moon to eastward rises pale and cool.

Rose and green around her, silver-gray and pearly,
Chequered with the black rooks flying home to bed;
For, to wake at daybreak, birds must couch them early:
And the day's a long one since the dawn was red.

On the chilly lakelet, in that pleasant gloaming,
See the sad swans sailing: they shall have no rest:
Never a voice to greet them save the bittern's booming
Where the ghostly sallows sway against the West.

'Sister,' saith the gray swan, 'Sister, I am weary,'
Turning to the white swan wet, despairing eyes;
'O' she saith, 'my young one! O' she saith, 'my dearie!'
Casts her wings about him with a storm of cries.

Woe for Lir's sweet children whom their vile stepmother
Glamoured with her witch-spells for a thousand years;
Died their father raving, on his throne another,
Blind before the end came from the burning tears.

Long the swans have wandered over lake and river;
Gone is all the glory of the race of Lir:
Gone and long forgotten like a dream of fever:
But the swans remember the sweet days that were.

Hugh, the black and white swan with the beauteous feathers,
Fiachra, the black swan with the emerald breast,
Conn, the youngest, dearest, sheltered in all weathers,
Him his snow-white sister loves the tenderest.

These her mother gave her as she lay a-dying;
To her faithful keeping; faithful hath she been,
With her wings spread o'er them when the tempest's crying,
And her songs so hopeful when the sky's serene.

Other swans have nests made 'mid the reeds and rushes,
Lined with downy feathers where the cygnets sleep
Dreaming, if a bird dreams, till the daylight blushes,
Then they sail out swiftly on the current deep.

With the proud swan-father, tall, and strong, and stately,
And the mild swan-mother, grave with household cares,
All well-born and comely, all rejoicing greatly:
Full of honest pleasure is a life like theirs.

But alas ! for my swans with the human nature,
Sick with human longings, starved for human ties,
With their hearts all human cramped to a bird's stature.
And the human weeping in the bird's soft eyes.

Never shall my swans build nests in some green river,
Never fly to Southward in the autumn gray,
Rear no tender children, love no mates for ever;
Robbed alike of bird's joys and of man's are they.

Babbles Conn the youngest, 'Sister, I remember
At my father's palace how I went in silk,
Ate the juicy deer-flesh roasted from the ember,
Drank from golden goblets my child's draught of milk.

Once I rode a-hunting, laughed to see the hurry,
Shouted at the ball-play, on the lake did row;
You had for your beauty gauds that shone so rarely.'
'Peace' saith Fionnuala, 'that was long ago.'

'Sister,' saith Fiachra, 'well do I remember
How the flaming torches lit the banquet-hall,
And the fire leapt skyward in the mid-December,
And among the rushes slept our staghounds tall.

By our father's right hand you sat shyly gazing,
Smiling half and sighing, with your eyes a-glow,
As the bards sang loudly all your beauty praising.'
'Peace,' saith Fionnuala, 'that was long ago.'

'Sister,' then saith Hugh 'most do I remember
One I called my brother, one, earth's goodliest man,
Strong as forest oaks are where the wild vines clamber,
First at feast or hunting, in the battle's van.

Angus, you were handsome, wise, and true, and tender,
Loved by every comrade, feared by every foe:
Low, low, lies your beauty, all forgot your splendour.'
'Peace,' saith Fionnuala, 'that was long ago.'

Dews are in the clear air and the roselight paling;
Over sands and sedges shines the evening star;
And the moon's disc lonely high in heaven is sailing;
Silvered all the spear-heads of the rushes are.

Housed warm are all things as the night grows colder,
Water-fowl and sky-fowl dreamless in the nest;
But the swans go drifting, drooping wing and shoulder
Cleaving the still water where the fishes rest.

The Bird's Bargain
'O spare my cherries in the net,'
Brother Benignus prayed; 'and I
Summer and winter, shine and wet,
Will pile the blackbirds' table high.'

'O spare my youngling peas,' he prayed,
'That for the Abbot's table be;
And every blackbird shall be fed;
Yea, they shall have their fill,' said he.

His prayer, his vow, the blackbirds heard,
And spared his shining garden-plot.
In abstinence went every bird,
All the old thieving ways forgot.

He kept his promise to his friends,
And daily set them finest fare
Of corn and meal and manchet-ends,
With marrowy bones for winter bare.

Brother Benignus died in grace:
The brethren keep his trust, and feed
The blackbirds in this pleasant place,
Purged, as dear heaven, from strife and greed.

The blackbirds sing the whole year long,
Here where they keep their promise given,
And do the mellowing fruit no wrong.
Brother Benignus smiles in heaven.

The Truce Of God
After Suvla

Now to the stricken doe
And the wounded hind
There comes the Mercy of God
That is cool and kind.

To the hapless creature He made
He giveth rest.
All the woes of the world
Lie on His breast.

The tender Physician giveth
The drug of sleep,
Lest that His dove, His daughter,
Awake and weep.

Beyond all dreams of delight
Is the quiet peace,
He carries His lamb in His arms,
The blood on her fleece.

Wings In The Night

Now in the soft spring midnight
There's rush of wings and whirr,
Birds flying softly, swiftly;
The night's a-flutter, a-stir.

Home by the bitter seas,
They have sped home together.
So glad to be coming home
To the grey hills, the grey weather.

Calling and calling softly
One lights by the window-pane:
The rook, weary with building,
Turns to his sleep again.

Ere ever the moor-hens wake
And the wild duck come in,
The birds are about the house
With a long call and thin.

They have wakened the wood-pigeon
To make her plaintive moan,
The wood-pigeon lamenting
For sorrows not her own.

Oh, they are never birds,
But souls of men on the wind,
Seeking the mother's breast,
The heart that is soft and kind.

Souls of the Irish dead,
Flown from the fields of slaughter,
Home to the mother's arms
Over the wild grey water.

The Temple

What of Louvain and of Rheims
Made for God by man? What then?

Here be temples more than man's
Wrought by God for His own men.

Scattered in the rain and frost,
Marred of beauty, there they be,
Temples of the Holy Ghost,
Broken, ruined piteously.

Bodies all so finely wrought,
Cunning deftness shaped them well;
These, God's ultimate, loving thought
For His Spirit's citadel.

Beautiful from head to foot,
Young, dear darlings all unflawed
For their mother's kiss. What brute
Dares deface the image of God?

Oh, the Temple's down! all marred
Gay and golden boys must lie:
Bitter-sweet as spikenard
Is the old name we called them by.

Hush! God's Temple in its fall
Breaks to set the spirit free
From the golden cage and thrall.
Into heaven-winged liberty.

From the cage the bird is flown,
Sings so high above our sphere.
Hush, be never a sigh or moan:
The fledged bird flies without fear.

All our loves are gathered in,
Every gay and golden lad;
On new raiment, white and clean,
They behold God and are glad.

A Gardener Sage
Here in the garden-bed,
Hoeing the celery,
Wonders the Lord has made
Pass ever before me.
I see the young birds build,
And swallows come and go,
And summer grow and gild,
And winter die in snow.

Many a thing I note,

And store it in my mind,
For all my ragged coat
That scarce will stop the wind.
I light my pipe and draw,
And, leaning on my spade,
I marvel with much awe
O'er all the Lord hath made.

Now, here's a curious thing:
Upon the first of March
The crow goes house-building
In the elm and in the larch.
And be it shine or snow,
Though many winds carouse,
That day the artful crow
Begins to build his house.

But then—the wonder's big!
If Sunday fell that day,
Nor straw, nor screw, nor twig,
Till Monday would he lay.
His black wings to his side,
He'd drone upon his perch,
Subdued and holy-eyed
As though he were in church.

The crow's a gentleman
Not greatly to my mind,
He'll steal what seeds he can,
And all you hide he'll find.
Yet though he's bully and sneak,
To small birds, bird of prey,
He counts the days of the week,
And keeps the Sabbath Day.

Winter Sunset
Roses in the sky,
Roses in the sea
Bowers of scarlet sky-roses
Take my heart and me.

God was good to make,
This December weather,
All this sky a rose-garden,
Rose and fire together.

To the East are burning
Roses in a garden,
Roses in a rosy field,
Hesper for their warden.

Yonder to the West
Roses all afire,
Mirror now some rare splendid
Rose of their desire.

Pulsing deeper, deeper,
Waves of fire throb on,
Never were such red roses
At sunset or dawn.

Roses on the hills,
Roses in the hollow,
Roses on the wet hedges,
In the shining fallow.

West wind, blow and blow!
That has blown ajar
Gates of God's great rose-garden,
Where His Angels are,

Gathering up the rose-leaves
For a shower of roses
On the night the Lord Babe
His sweet eye uncloses.

All the sky is scarlet
Flaming on the azure.
O, there's fire in Heaven
My heart aches with pleasure.

Leagues of rose and scarlet,
Roses red as blood:
All the world's a rose-garden.
God is good, is good.

The Dead Coach
At night when sick folk wakeful lie,
I heard the dead coach passing by,
And heard it passing wild and fleet,
And knew my time was come not yet.

Click-clack, click-clack, the hoofs went past,
Who takes the dead coach travels fast,
On and away through the wild night,
The dead must rest ere morning light.

If one might follow on its track
The coach and horses, midnight black,
Within should sit a shape of doom

That beckons one and all to come.

God pity them to-night who wait
To hear the dead coach at their gate,
And him who hears, though sense be dim,
The mournful dead coach stop for him.

He shall go down with a still face,
And mount the steps and take his place,
The door be shut, the order said!
How fast the pace is with the dead!

Click-clack, click-clack, the hour is chill,
The dead coach climbs the distant hill.
Now, God, the Father of us all,
Wipe Thou the widow's tears that fall!

The Refuge
I will lift mine eyes to the mountains,
To the mountains whence cometh my aid;
I shall drink of the Mercy's crystal fountains,
And shall not be afraid.

St. Patrick and St. Bride be with me,
And all the saints of the Gael;
The wings of Heaven above and beneath me,
The dead of Inisfail.

The caves of the mountains shall receive me,
I shall lie as at a mother's breast
The white food the King of Heaven shall give me,
And the wine of Heaven for feast.

Where the eagle screams over Nephin,
Where the Reek of Patrick looks on the isles,
li-orn the voices of the world that fret and deafen,
From the evil in her smiles,

I shall creep, and the mountains will hold me,
As a lamb that runs with the ewe,
The warmth of the mother shall enfold me,
I shall have milk and dew.

Nymphs
Where are ye now, O beautiful girls of the mountain,
Oreads all ?
Nothing at all stirs here save the drip of the fountain;
Answers our call
Only the heart-glad thrush, in the Vale of Thrushes;

Stirs in the brake
But the dew-bright ear of the hare in his couch of rushes
Listening, awake.

Blessings
God bless the little orchard brown
Where the sap stirs these quickening days.
Soon in a white and rosy gown
The trees will give great praise.

God knows I have it in my mind,
The white house with the golden eaves.
God knows since it is left behind
That something grieves and grieves.

God keep the small house in his care,
The garden bordered all in box,
Where primulas and wallflowers are
And crocuses in flocks.

God keep the little rooms that ope
One to another, swathed in green,
Where honeysuckle lifts her cup
With jessamine between.

God bless the quiet old grey head
That dreams beside the fire of me,
And makes home there for me indeed
Over the Irish Sea.

The Doves
The house where I was born,
Where I was young and gay,
Grows old amid its corn,
Amid its scented hay.

Moan of the cushat dove,
In silence rich and deep;
The old head I love
Nods to its quiet sleep.

Where once were nine and ten
Now two keep house together;
The doves moan and complain
All day in the still weather.

What wind, bitter and great,
Has swept the country's face,
Altered, made desolate

The heart-remembered place?

What wind, bitter and wild,
Has swept the towering trees
Beneath whose shade a child
Long since gathered heartease?

Under the golden eaves
The house is still and sad,
As though it grieves and grieves
For many a lass and lad.

The cushat doves complain
All day in the still weather;
Where once were nine or ten
But two keep house together.

Slow Spring
O year, grow slowly. Exquisite, holy,
The days go on
With almonds showing the pink stars blowing
And birds in the dawn.

Grow slowly, year, like a child that is dear,
Or a lamb that is mild,
By little steps, and by little skips,
Like a lamb or a child.

The Foggy Dew
A splendid place is London, with golden store,
For them that have the heart and hope and youth galore;
But mournful are its streets to me, I tell you true,
For I'm longing sore for Ireland in the foggy dew.

The sun he shines all day here, so fierce and fine,
With never a wisp of mist at all to dim his shine;
The sun he shines all day here from skies of blue:
He hides his face in Ireland in the foggy dew.

The maids go out to milking in the pastures gray,
The sky is green and golden at dawn of the day;
And in the deep-drenched meadows the hay lies new,
And the corn is turning yellow in the foggy dew.

Mavrone! if I might feel now the dew on my face,
And the wind from the mountains in that remembered place,
I'd give the wealth of London, if mine it were to do,
And I'd travel home to Ireland and the foggy dew.

The Broken Soldier

The broken soldier sings and whistles day to dark;
He's but the remnant of a man, maimed and half-blind,
But the soul they could not harm goes singing like the lark,
Like the incarnate Joy that will not be confined.

The Lady at the Hall has given him a light task,
He works in the gardens as busy as a bee;
One hand is but a stump and his face a pitted mask;
The gay soul goes singing like a bird set free.

Whistling and singing like a linnet on wings;
The others stop to listen, leaning on the spade,
Whole men and comely, they fret at little things.
The soul of him's singing like a thrush in a glade.

Hither and thither, hopping, like Robin on the grass,
The soul in the broken man is beautiful and brave;
And while he weeds the pansies and the bright hours pass
The bird caught in the cage whistles its joyous stave.

The Heroes

By such strange and wonderful ways
God would save His world again.
All our days are holy days,
Starry heroes all our men.

There's naught common or unclean
In this splendid new-made earth:
Hearts uplifted, eyes serene,
Grief goes gayer now than mirth.

Quietly in the sacred night
Tears must fall, O noble tears!
That are shed in the Lords' sight
And are only for His ears.

Who would mourn aloud for sons
Gorgeous in our firmament,
Starry constellations
In the way their fathers went?

From the innumerable grave
There will spring a world new-born,
With the austerest eyes and brave
And its clear gaze towards the morn.

He who gave His Son to die

For man's purchase, gives once more
These, His beloved sons, to buy
Him a world worth dying for.

What Turned The Germans Back
What turned the German myriads back
From Paris wh ther they had won?
The sword dropped from their hold grown slack;
Children of Attila the Hun,
Like Attila, went backward driven
By a young shepherdess of Heaven.

A shepherdess is Genevieve,
And though her flock should wander light,
This shepherdess is quick to save
The black, the speckled and the white.
She takes her golden crook and goes
And deals destruction to its foes.

She who turned Attila back, so slim,
A shepherdess that keeps the flock,
Waited as once she did for him,
Slight as a reed or her own crook;
"Turn back in God's Name!" They went back.
The tide is stemmed for her sweet sake.

White Genevieve upon her hill
Prays, and the German hosts retreat.
She plucks the Robes of Heaven still
That Heaven give victory for defeat;
And keeps her motley flock in sight,
The black, the speckled and the white.

A Prayer (For Those Who Shall Return)
Lord, when they come back again
From the dreadful battlefield
To the common ways of men,
Be Thy mercy, Lord, revealed!
Make them to forget the dread
Fields of dying and the dead!

Let them go unhaunted, Lord,
By the sights that they have seen:
Guard their dreams from shell and sword;
Lead them by the pastures green,
That they wander all night long
In the fields where they were young.

Grant no charnel horrors slip

'Twixt them and their child's soft face.
Breast to breast and lip to lip,
Let the lovers meet, embrace!
Be they innocent of all
Memories that affright, appal.

Let their ears love music still,
And their eyes rejoice to see
Glory on the sea and hill,
Beauty in the flower and tree.
Drop a veil that none may raise
Over dreadful nights and days.

A Song For The New Year (1915)
The Year of the Sorrows went out with great wind:
Lift up, lift up, O broken hearts, your Lord is kind,
And He shall call His flock home where no storms be
Into a sheltered haven out of sound of the sea.

There shall be bright sands there and a milken hill,
They shall lie in the sun there and drink their fill,
They shall have dew and shade there and grass to the knee,
Safe in a sheltered haven out of sound of the sea.

He shall bind their wounds up and their tears shall cease:
They shall have sweetest pillows and a bed of ease.
Come up, come up and hither, O little flock, saith He,
Ye shall have sheltered havens out of sound of the sea.

The first day of New Year strewed the sea with dead.
Lift up, lift up, O broken heart and hanging head!
The Lord walks on the waters and a Shepherd is He
They shall have sheltered havens out of sound of the sea.

Any Mother
'What's the news? Now tell it me.'
'Allenby again advances.'
'No, it is not Allenby
But my boy, straight as a lance is.

'Oh, my boy it is that runs,
Hurls his young and slender body
On the dread death-dealing guns.
Oh, he's down! his head is bloody!'

'Haig's offensive has begun.'
'Say not Haig's nor any other,
Since it is my one sweet son
In the gases' risk and smother.

'He is taken by the throat,
In the bursting flame will quiver,
He the billet for all shot,
He the shell's objective ever.'

So not Allenby nor Haig,
But her darling goes to battle.
All the world's red mist and vague
Shattered by the scream and rattle.

Just one slender shape she sees,
One bright head tossed hither, thither;
Oh, if he goes down the seas
Whelm her and the world together!

All Souls
There's traffic in the worlds immortal,
For many souls are flying home,
Striving and pushing at the portal
For sight of glorious things to come.

What rout of wings against the sunset?
What rosy plumes the dawning bar?
Heaven's stormed with gay and happy onset
Of youngling things home from the War.

Against the inverted cup of azure,
Against the evening, peach and green,
The frolicsome young souls take their pleasure,
Darting the silver stars between.

Though the old nests be sad, forsaken,
The cotes of Heaven are yet unfilled:
In trees of Heaven as yet untaken
The immortal Loves lift hearts and build.

Christmas In The Year Of The War
Nevertheless this Year of Grief
The Tree of God's in leaf.

The stem, the branch quickeneth
With sap, this year of Death.

For in the time of the flowering thorn
The Babe, the Babe, is born!

Christ's folk, look up, be not dismayed,
The Lord's in the cattle shed.

He comes, a little trembling One,
To a world else lost, undone.

With His poor folk He wills to stay
In this their difficult day.

Poor war-worn world, you shall have ease!
He signs your lasting peace.

He hath given His people rest from wars,
By the cold light of stars.

The charter of their peace shall stand
Writ by His hour-old hand.

The Tree of Paradise quickeneth.
Be still, there is no death!

Easter
Bring flowers to strew His way,
Yea, sing, make holiday;
Bid young lambs leap,
And earth laugh after sleep.

For now He cometh forth
Winter flies to the north,
Folds wings and cries
Amid the bergs and ice.

Yea, Death, great Death is dead,
And Life reigns in his stead;
Cometh the Athlete
New from dead Death's defeat.

Cometh the Wrestler,
But Death he makes no stir,
Utterly spent and done,
And all his kingdom gone.

Good Friday, A.D. 33
Mother, why are people crowding now and staring?
Child, it is a malefactor goes to His doom,
To the high hill of Calvary He's faring,
And the people pressing and pushing to make room
Lest they miss the sight to come.

Oh, the poor malefactor, heavy is His load!
Now He falls beneath it and they goad Him on.

Sure the road to Calvary's a steep up-hill road
Is there none to help Him with His Cross - not one?
Must He bear it all alone?

Here is a country boy with business in the city,
Smelling of the cattle's breath and the sweet hay;
Now they bid him lift the Cross, so they have some pity:
Child, they fear the malefactor dies on the way
And robs them of their play.

Has He no friends then, no father nor mother,
None to wipe the sweat away nor pity His fate?
There's a woman weeping and there's none to soothe her:
Child, it is well the seducer expiate
His crimes that are so great.

Mother, did I dream He once bent above me,
This poor seducer with the thorn-crowned head,
His hands on my hair and His eyes seemed to love me?
Suffer little children to come to Me, He said
His hair, his brows drip red.

Hurrying through Jerusalem on business or pleasure
People hardly pause to see Him go to His death
Whom they held five days ago more than a King's treasure,
Shouting Hosannas, flinging many a wreath
For this Jesus of Nazareth.

Resurrection
Now the golden daffodil
Lifts from earth his shining head
That was lately frozen still
In the gardens of the dead.

Sing to the Lord a new song!
Roundelays and virelays,
Who hath slain Death and is young
Master of your holidays.

Now from places underground
Gold and purple folk will go
Haled by the shrill trumpet sound
From their wormy beds below.

Now the stone is from the tomb!
Now 'tis Easter and the morn!
Christ the Lord of Life is come,
Hath slain Death, and Life is born.

Christ the Lord of Life new-risen,

Calls the sleepers that they rise
From the unnumbered graves, break prison,
Follow Him to Paradise.

Who be then these shining ones
Dancing with a heavenly mirth,
The King's daughters, the King's sons,
Fairer than the folk of earth?

Graves are busier than a hive
The wind blows, the sun is warm;
Now the dead are come alive
Loosed is many a golden swarm.

Sing to the Lord a new song!
The Sun's risen in our East;
Christ the Lord of Life is young.
And the young sit to the feast.

The Deserted
Thou Who wert kindest of the kind
Since out of sight is out of mind
There's none to do Thee kindnesses
In Thy last anguish and distress.
Thou art left all alone, alone.
Where are Thy faithful lovers flown?

Where is the multitude that fed,
With loaves and fishes comfortèd?
The blind Thou mad'st to see? the lame
That walked? the one leper who came
Of nine made clean? The dumb that spoke?
Where are they - all Thy loving folk?

How is it they have naught to say?
Where's Lazarus risen from the clay?
Where is the widow of Nain? where
Jairus's daughter, small and fair?
Judas has sold Thee to Thy foes,
And Peter weeps while the cock crows.

Simon will help Thee on Thy road
Unwillingly ah, Lamb of God!
Thou bearest the world's weight up that hill,
And none to help Thee with good will;
Stumbling and falling, while Thy hurt
Makes for the rabble noble sport.

But yet there's balm in Gilead,
For here's His Mother, sweet and sad,

Here's Magdalen weeping, and with them
The women of Jerusalem;
They have run all the way since one
Brought them the news: He's not alone!

Veronica is nothing loth
To wipe His poor face with her cloth.
His Mother's by Him and St. John,
With many a starry legion;
Magdalen's hair is round His feet,
Her tears wash off the blood and sweat.

Thou Who wert kindest of the kind,
Though out of sight be out of mind
Thou art not forgot: by land and sea
The broken hearts come home to Thee,
And bear Thine anguish and Thy grief
Till the Third Day shall bring relief.

Joining The Colours
There they go marching all in step so gay!
Smooth-cheeked and golden, food for shells and guns.
Blithely they go as to a wedding day,
The mothers' sons.

The drab street stares to see them row on row
On the high tram-tops, singing like the lark.
Too careless-gay for courage, singing they go
Into the dark.

With tin whistles, mouth-organs, any noise,
They pipe the way to glory and the grave;
Foolish and young, the gay and golden boys
Love cannot save.

High heart! High courage! The poor girls they kissed
Run with them : they shall kiss no more, alas!
Out of the mist they stepped-into the mist

The Colonists
To men now of her blood and race
England's a little garden place,
Dear as a woman is, and she
The Queen of every loyalty.

To dwellers 'mid the ice and snows,
She is their secret garden rose
From which that bee, their heart, sucks off
For the cold Winter honey enough.

To toilers 'mid the sultry plains,
Sick for her tempered suns and rains,
She is the thought that wets their eyes
And hearts with dew of Paradise.

Most loved of those who never knew
Her green o' the silk and her soft blue,
Her mild inviolate fields that be
Hedged with the sweet-briar of the sea.

Sweet in their dreams her Summers are,
Her tranquil nights of moon and star,
The love-songs of her nightingales;
A water-spring that never fails.

Amid their unending distances
Her little crowded sweetness is
A dream of rest, a dream of prayer,
With homes and children everywhere.

Touch her - and they are all on fire,
This little land of their desire
Seen in a mirage far away
With light upon her night and day.

No Man's Land
Not to an angel but a friend
He turned at the day's bitter end.
It was so comforting to feel
Some one was near, to see him kneel
By the deep shell-hole's edge: to know
He was not left to the fierce foe.

This soldier who had eased his head
And staunched the flow where it had bled,
Who made a pillow of his breast
Where the poor tossing head might rest,
Wore a young face he used to know
Yesterday, some time, long ago.

The night's cold it was bitter enough,
But who shall keep the fierce Day off?
And must he lie, be burnt and baked
In the hot sands, with lips unslaked?
Will no one give him dews and rain?
Lord, send the frozen night again!

But here's the one who comforted!
No angel, but a boy instead,

Slender and young, above him leans:
The sands are changed to tender greens;
He hears the wind in the sycamore
Sing a low song by his mother's door.

Such tender touches to his wound,
Such loving arms to clasp him round,
Until they find him the third day!
The stretcher-bearers heard him say,
Don't leave me, Denis! I am here.'
Denis? But Denis died last year!

He will maintain that Denis was
Beside him in his bitter case,
Denis more beautiful and gay
Than in the dear, remembered day:
God sent no angel, but a friend
To save him at the bitter end.

Dead - A Prisoner
He died the loneliest death of all,
Amid his foes he died.
But Someone's leaped the outer wall
And Someone s come inside,
And he has gotten a golden key
To set the lonesome prisoner free.

It was not Peter with the keys,
The heavenly janitor,
Who has passed them like a rushing breeze,
The gaolers at the door,
And to His bosom as a bed
Has taken the unmothered head.

A great light in the prison shone
That made the people blind:
Rise up, rise up, new-ransomed one,
And taste the sun and wind:
For I have gotten a golden key
To set all lonesome prisoners free.

Yea they shall soar, shall spring aloft;
Their gyves shall not be rough,
But just the links of love, so soft
That they shall not cast off.
Rise up, my dear, and come away.'
And they went out to the great day.

The Great Chance

Now strikes the hour upon the clock
The black sheep may rebuild the years
May lift the father's pride he broke
And wipe away his mother's tears.

To him, the mark for thrifty scorn;
God hath another chance to give,
Sets in his heart a flame new-born
By which his muddied soul may live.

This is the day of the prodigal,
The decent people's shame and grief,
When he shall make amends for all.
The way to Glory's bloody and brief.

Clean from his baptism, of blood,
New from the fire he springs again,
In shining raiment white and good,
Beyond the wise, home-keeping man.

Somewhere to-night-no tears be shed!-
With shaking hands they turn the sheet
To find his name among the dead,
Flower of the Army and the Fleet.

They tell, with proud and stricken face,
Of his white boyhood far away-
Who talked of trouble or disgrace?
'Our splendid son is dead!' they say.

The Comrades
The angels walk with men in the red ruin and rain,
White and gold, as of old, without spot or stain.
Our warriors fought and died, the white lords by their side.
The angels walk with men.

God doth not forget in the battle, the retreat;
The heart of Love's above the dying and the slain.
There's a ladder to the skies and, armed from Paradise,
The angels walk with men.

Foot-soldiers, cavaliers, the flame on their spears,
They sweep fast in haste o'er the bloody plain.
What ill shall betide us with the winged knights beside us?
The angels walk with men.

Golden-mailed, lance in arm, they ride on the storm
Michael and a poor soldier are comrades twain!
Oh, in the noise of battle, the red roar and the rattle,
The angels walk with men!

The Fields Of France
Jesus Christ they chased away
Comes again another day.
Could they do without Him then
His poor lost unhappy men?
He returns and is revealed
In the trenches and the field.

Where the dead lie thick He goes,
Where the brown earth's red as a rose,
He who walked the waters wide
Treads the wine-press, purple-dyed,
Stoops, and bids the piteous slain
That they rise with Him again.

To His breast and in his cloak
Bears the younglings of the flock:
Calls His poor sheep to come home
And His sheep rise up and come.
They shall rest by a clear pool
'Mid the pastures beautiful!

Jesus Christ they chased away
Has come back another day.

Menace
Oh, when the land is white as milk
With bloom that lets no leaf between,
When trees are clad in grass-green silk
And thrushes sing in a gold screen:
What is it ails Dark Rosaleen?

Why is the banshee in the night
Crying for all the young men gone?
Now when the world with bloom is white,
When the good sun's warm on the stone,
Why does the Woman of Death make moan?

As one who is not comforted,
I heard in every lonely glen
Dark Rosaleen cry for her dead
And for her dying race of men.
Dark Rosaleen, take heart again!

For, oh, there's God in His high place
And Patrick seated by His side
To judge with Him the Irish race;
And Columcille, Kieran and Bride

Shall not forget before God's Face.

There's Mary of the Seven Swords,
Queen of the Gael - oh, many a saint,
With Oliver Plunkett to look towards
The Mercy Seat, with praise and plaint,
For Rosaleen, ever the Lord's.

Oh, weep no more, Dark Rosaleen!
Menace and terror pass you by.
Oh, loved beyond the sceptred queen,
Dark Rosaleen for whom men die!
And loved till death, Dark Rosaleen.

Indian Summer
This is the sign!
This flooding splendour, golden and hyaline,
This sun a golden sea on hill and plain,
That God forgets not, that He walks with men.
His smile is on the mountain and the pool
And all the fairy lakes are beautiful.
This is the word!
That makes a thing of flame the water-bird.
This mercy of His fulfilled in the magical
Clear glow of skies from dawn to evenfall,
Telling His Hand is over us, that we
Are not delivered to the insatiable sea.
This is the pledge!
The promise writ in gold to the water's edge:
His bow's in Heaven and the great floods are over.
Oh, broken hearts, lift up! The Immortal Lover
Embraces, comforts with the enlivening sun,
The sun He bids stand still till the day is won.

High Summer
Pinks and syringa in the garden closes
And the sweet privet hedge and golden roses.
The pines hot in the sun, the drone of the bee;
They die in Flanders to keep these for me.

The long sunny days and the still weather,
The cuckoo and the blackbird shouting together,
The lambs calling their mothers out on the lea;
They die in Flanders to keep these for me.

The doors and windows open: South wind blowing
Warm through the clean sweet rooms, on tip-toe going,
Where many sanctities, dear and delightsome be
They die in Flanders to keep these for me.

Daisies leaping in foam on the green grasses,
The dappled sky and the stream that sings as it passes
These are bought with a price, a bitter fee
They die in Flanders to keep these for me.

The Broken Soldier
The broken soldier sings and whistles day to dark;
He's but the remnant of a man, maimed and half-blind,
But the soul they could not harm goes singing like the lark,
Like the incarnate Joy that will not be confined.

The Lady at the Hall has given him a light task,
He works in the gardens as busy as a bee;
One hand is but a stump and his face a pitted mask;
The gay soul goes singing like a bird set free.

Whistling and singing like a linnet on wings;
The others stop to listen, leaning on the spade,
Whole men and comely, they fret at little things.
The soul of him's singing like a thrush in a glade.

Hither and thither, hopping, like Robin on the grass,
The soul in the broken man is beautiful and brave;
And while he weeds the pansies and the bright hours pass
The bird caught in the cage whistles its joyous stave.

The Lowlands Of Flanders
The night that I was married
Our Captain came to me:
Rise up, rise up, new-married man
And come at once with me.

For the Lowlands of Flanders,
It's there that we must fight;
So look your last and buss your last,
For we shall sail to-night.

'Tis all for our Counterie
And for our King we go
To the Lowlands of Flanders
Against the German foe.

The girl that weds a soldier
Must never blench for fear;
I kissed my last and looked my last
Upon my lovely dear.

The Lowlands of Flanders,

Their rivers run so red.
But I must say Good-bye, my dear,
My only dear, I said.

For now I must go sailing
Upon the stormy main;
Good-bye, good-bye, my only Love,
Till I shall come again.

I put her white arms from me,
Her cheek was cold as clay.
The night that I was married
No longer I might stay.

Our bugles they are blowing,
And I must sail the sea,
For the Lowlands of Flanders
Betwixt my love and me.

Immortality
So I have sunk my roots in earth
Since that my pretty boys had birth;
And fear no more the grave and gloom,
I, with the centuries to come.

As the tree blossoms so bloom I,
Flinging wild branches to the sky;
Renew each year my leafy suit,
Strike with the years a deeper root.

Shelter a thousand birds to be,
A thousand herds give praise to me;
And in my kind and grateful shade
How many a weary head be laid.

I clothe myself without a stain.
In me a child is born again,
A child that looks with innocent eyes
On a new world with glad surprise.

The old mistakes are all undone,
All the old sins are purged and gone.
Old wounds and scars have left no trace,
There are no lines in this young face.

To hear the cuckoo the first time,
And 'mid new roses in the prime
To read the poets newly. This,
Year after year, shall be my bliss.

Of me shall love be born anew;
I shall be loved and lover too;
Years after this poor body has died
Shall be the bridegroom and the bride.

Of me shall mothers spring to know
The mother's bliss, the mother's woe;
And children's children yet to be
Shall learn their prayers about my knee.

And many million lights of home
Shall light for me the time to come.
Unto me much shall be forgiven,
I that make many souls for heaven.

The Old Soldier
Lest the young soldiers be strange in heaven,
God bids the old soldier they all adored
Come to Him and wait for them, clean, new-shriven,
A happy doorkeeper in the House of the Lord.

Lest it abash them, the strange new splendour,
Lest it affright them, the new robes clean;
Here's an old face, now, long-tried, and tender,
A word and a hand-clasp as they troop in.

'My boys,' he greets them: and heaven is homely,
He their great captain in days gone o'er;
Dear is the friend's face, honest and comely,
Waiting to welcome them by the strange door.

Mediation
If Thou, Lord God, willest to judge
This, Thy very piteous clay
Which to save Christ did not grudge
His last dying, I shall say:
Lord, I interpose Christ's death
'Twixt these children and Thy wrath.

Then if Thou shouldst say: Their shame
Is as scarlet in Mine eyes
I shall ask: Who took their blame?
Look, Lord, on this Sacrifice!
Is Thy Son's blood not more bright
Which hath washed their scarlet white?

Then, if Thou Thy wrath should'st keep
And Thy gaze should'st still avert
From Thy Son s most piteous sheep,

I shall ask: Who bare the hurt?
I Present Christ's death and Pain
'Twixt Thine anger and these men.

Lord, they die by millions
And they look to Thee take thought!
This dear flock, that is Thy Son's,
By the richest ransom bought.
See, Thy dead Son lies between,
Thee, the High Judge, and their sin.

Emptiness
Where there is nothing God comes in:
The Very God has room enough
In the poor heart that's stripped so clean
Of earth and all the joys thereof.

I looked for shadow and the night
When Death had taken her Love away,
But for the darkness there was light,
And for the night clear floods of day.

Great light that filled it to the brim
And overflowed and spilt around,
Flowing from Him, pulsing from Him,
And all the heart was holy ground.

The earth, the heavens, cannot contain
Our God, nor any starry place;
But He who takes delight with men
Bounds Him within a narrow space.

And where her poor heart bleeds and breaks
Because her dearest Love is dead,
The Lord of Life comes in and takes
Warm to His arms the piteous head.

The Image
When a wild grace I see,
A turn o' the neck, a curl, sweet hands, clear eyes,
Gentleness, courtesy, dignity;
In all these gifts Thee I surmise, surprise.

All beauty and delight.
Skin like a rose, a beauteous shape, an air
Free and enchanting, give my weary sight
Glimpses of Thee, Thou Beauty past compare.

Strength, courage also are Thine.

And joy of youth and wings that cleave the blue,
Low singing and soft voices, I divine
In these Thy beauty ancient yet ever new.

Oh, when my startled eye
Perceives this beauty league-long, sea and isle
And eagle-crested mountains wild and high,
I catch Thy Maker's thought - I see Thy smile.

Some mirror out of range
Flashes reflex of Heaven on this sweet earth,
Brooding forever, beautiful, without change,
The blue-bell sea, the thousand streams' soft mirth.

All beauty is of Thee.
Kindness and quietness, moon and stars and sun,
Gardens and woods, the bird in the new-fledged tree
And sleep, O Kindest One!

The Aerodrome
So now the aerodrome goes up
Upon my father's fields,
And gone is all the golden crop
And all the pleasant yields.

They tear the trees up, branch and root,
They kill the hedges green,
As though some force, malign and brute,
Ravaged the peace serene.

There where he used to sit and gaze
With blue and quiet eyes,
Watching his comely cattle graze,
The walls begin to rise.

What place for robin or for wren,
For thrush and blackbird's call?
Now there shall be but flying men
Nor any bird at all.

'Twas well he did not stay to know,
Defaced and all defiled
The quiet fields of long ago,
Dear to him as a child.

But when the tale was told to me
I felt such piercing pain,
They tore my heart up with the tree
That will not leaf again.

The New Recruit

The lads were once my comrades,
They stay at home content.
And now's the time of cricket,
They count the days well spent.

They walk with girls o' Sundays,
All in their Sunday clothes;
And of a Sunday evening
Go where good liquor flows.

Their way's no longer my way,
For I must follow now
The drum-tap and the bugle,
While they're for shop and plough.

Good-bye, good-bye, kind people,
And all I leave behind,
To girls that used to kiss me,
To one was never kind.

Good-bye, my girl unwilling,
I shall not vex you sore,
For I have taken the shilling
And I come home no more.

I heard the drums a-drumming,
And I ran out to see;
The soldiers and the fighting,
They mattered nought to me.

Good-bye, my girl that grieved me.
The bugles whistled, Come.
And I, stepped in the roadway
And marched beside the drum.

Lord, I was proud, uplifted.
I held my head so high;
And all the girls were doating
With love as we went by!

The boys who stood and jeered me
May live to three-score-ten,
While I'm cut down at morning
Among the fighting men.

But Lord, the people shouting!
The glory tasted sweet,
And the eyes of the girls all doating
As we marched down the street.

The Bird's Bargain

'O spare my cherries in the net,'
Brother Benignus prayed; 'and I
Summer and winter, shine and wet,
Will pile the blackbirds' table high.'

'O spare my youngling peas,' he prayed,
'That for the Abbot's table be;
And every blackbird shall be fed;
Yea, they shall have their fill,' said he.

His prayer, his vow, the blackbirds heard,
And spared his shining garden-plot.
In abstinence went every bird,
All the old thieving ways forgot.

He kept his promise to his friends,
And daily set them finest fare
Of corn and meal and manchet-ends,
With marrowy bones for winter bare.

Brother Benignus died in grace:
The brethren keep his trust, and feed
The blackbirds in this pleasant place,
Purged, as dear heaven, from strife and greed.

The blackbirds sing the whole year long,
Here where they keep their promise given,
And do the mellowing fruit no wrong.
Brother Benignus smiles in heaven.

Epiphany: (For Dora, 1918)

She carried frankincense and gold
When the Star guided her,
And in her folded hands so cold
She carried myrrh.

Frankincense for the praise she owed,
Gold for her gift was meet,
But myrrh because so oft her road
Was bitter-sweet.

Lay her tired body in that earth
Was holy to her mind!
But the bird-soul flies in high mirth,
Borne on the wind.

It tosses in the Irish skies

Awhile, so small and white,
Ere it is gone swiftly it flies
Into the light.

She has gone in with the Three Kings,
In silk and miniver;
The gold, the frankincense she brings,
The sharp-sweet myrrh.

Quiet Eyes
The boys come home, come home from war,
With quiet eyes for quiet things
A child, a lamb, a flower, a star,
A bird that softly sings.

Young faces war-worn and deep-lined,
The satin smoothness past recall;
Yet out of sight is out of mind
For the worst wrong of all.

As nightmare dreams that pass with sleep,
The horror and grief intolerable.
The unremembering young eyes keep
Their innocence. All is well!

The worldling's eyes are dusty dim,
The eyes of sin are weary and cold,
The fighting boy brings home with him
The unsullied eyes of old.

The war has furrowed the young face.
Oh, there's no all-heal, no wound-wort!
The soul looks from its hidden place
Unharmed, unflawed, unhurt.

The Great Sorrow
Voice of a great wind, of wild ocean surges,
Storming the gates of Heaven,
The people of God singing under the scourges
Wherewith they are healed and shriven.

This is no sound, no wail of lamentation
Such as of old was heard
When Rachael cried to Heaven her desolation
Until all Heaven was stirred.

The people sing, crushed in the wine-press ruddy,
Broken but not dismayed,
The triumph-song of the soul over the body

Heaven-lifted, angel-stayed.

The white sorrow homes to the heavenly portal.
This grief, this grief has wings
Blood on her breast, but through the groves immortal
Her song of triumph rings.

Colours
Blues and greens are my delight
Set in garlands of the white.

When God made the violet
He made nothing better yet.

Lilac and the lavender
Fit for queens of Heaven to wear.

Many russets and the rose,
God be praised for these and those!

For the silvers and the greys
Likewise ye shall give Him praise.

Scarlet is a King's colour
That the King of Kings once wore.

Yet when everything is said,
Bring me neither rose nor red.

Give me blue and green below,
Apple bloom and cherry snow.

Blue forget-me-nots beneath
Pear and plum-bloom in a wreath.

Or wild hyacinths in a glade
Nothing better God has made.

Blues and greens and a white bough
Turn the earth to Heaven now.

Mid The Piteous Heaps Of Dead
'Mid the piteous heaps of dead
Goes one weary golden head
Tossing ever to and fro,
Calling loud and calling low.

Mother, mother, step so light,
Mother, lay your fingers white

On my forehead like a dew!
Mother, mother, where are you?

Still so loud he makes his cry
That the dying cannot die;
All the writhing field's one groan
While he lies and cries alone.

But his mother's far away;
Cannot hear him cry and say:
Mother, I am dying, come!
Mother, I am lost from home!

Mary, Mother of all men,
Come and comfort him in pain.
Take his young head to the breast
Where your Child and God had rest.

Mary, Mary, step so light.
Mary, lay your fingers white
On his forehead! He shall dream
That his mother comforts him.

Mary, Mother, croon him o'er
Lullabies you sang before!
Mary, ease him, crooning low,
In the way that mothers know!

The Only Son
His mother died last year and yet
She wearied Heaven with fear and fret,
Wanting the son she left behind,
And God was patient, being kind.

He was so beautiful, so young,
Slender as a tall tree, wind-swung;
Innocent, gay: she went in fear
Something might hurt him, lacking her.

She heard amid the starry mirth
Rumour of dreadful things on earth.
Of sweet youth slain and beauty marred
Beyond all balm and spikenard.

Oh, had she visions of his plight
Lying in the red rain at night
Amid the piteous heap of slain,
That she was wild with fear and pain?

God gives His angels. But she went

Uncomforted and discontent.
Because no angel ever knew
The way to love that mothers do.

And so she wearied Heaven with prayer,
Her knees for ever on God's stair,
Her troubled thoughts forever abeat
Like wings about the Mercy-Seat.

At last God heard her. Swift as the wind
His messenger went forth to find
Her son and bring him to her breast
So that at last her heart might rest.

She died a year ago and still
Her cup of Heaven's untasted till
God's messenger returns to say:
'He fell in action yesterday.'

Palestine: 1917
How strange if it should fall to you,
To me, our boys should do the deed
The great Crusaders failed to do!
To win Christ's Sepulchre: to bleed,
So the immortal dream come true.

What ghosts now throng the Holy Ground,
With rusted armour, dinted sword,
Listening? The earth shakes with the sound;
The wind brings hither a fierce word:
To arms, to arms, Sons of Mahound!

In many a quiet cloister grey
Cross-legged Crusaders, men of stone,
Quiver and stir the Eastward way,
As they would spring up and be gone
To the Great Day, to the Great Day.

Godfrey and Lion-Heart and all
The splendours of the faithful years
Watch our young sons from the Knights' stall,
Ready to clap hands to their spears
If ill befall, if ill befall.

They say: It is the Child's Crusade
Was talked of in our early Spring.
St. George, St. Denis, to their aid!
That was a boy's voice challenging,
Shrill like a bugle, unafraid!

Most wonderful, if your son, my son,
Should win the Holy Thing at last!
The might of Heathenesse be undone,
The strong towers down, the gate unfast,
Lord Christ come to His own, His own.

Prayer At Night
Lord, for the one who dies alone
This night without companion,
I cannot rest, I cannot sleep.
O shepherd of the piteous sheep
Run with Thy crook, and lift in haste
The poor head to Thy loving breast.

Oh slake his deadly thirst from streams
Of Paradise, and give him dreams
Of the mild weather, the green sward.
Bind up his bitter wounds, O Lord,
And give him comfort. Let him know
His Shepherd 'tis that loves him so.

Thou countest Thy flock: not one is lost
But Thou goest seeking, for Thou knowest
The poor things creep away to die
Where none shall find save Thou art nigh.
Thou tak'st them to Thy arms, Thy knees,
And Thy sick lambs have sweetest ease.

Now I shall close my eyes in sleep,
Nor fret since they are Thine to keep,
Oh, happy sheep, to have such care,
The poorest, Love's own prisoner,
Who comforts as his mother might,
Rocking him into sleep at night.

The Promise
To you and you it shall be given,
As unto Mary her lost Heaven;
Her Son and your son come
Alive out of the grave and gloom.

Like hers your bliss is pre-ordained
To see the wounds healed and unstained;
Yea, you shall kiss with her
Where the sharp blade hath left no scar.

They shall come in warm to your cold
Dropped arms that found naught to enfold,
And on your heart be laid

The young, the beloved, thorn-crowned head.

Sudden some dawning or some eve
Your dead son shall come in alive,
As once came Mary's Son;
The lost, the incredible Heaven be won.

Lenton Communion
Rest in a friend's house, Dear, I pray:
The way is long to Good Friday,
And very chill and grey the way.

No crocus with its shining cup,
Nor the gold daffodil is up,
Nothing is here save the snowdrop.

Sit down with me and taste good cheer:
Too soon, too soon, Thy Passion's here;
The wind is keen and the skies drear.

Sit by my fire and break my bread.
Yea, from Thy dish may I be fed,
And under Thy feet my hair spread!

Lord, in the quiet, chill and sweet,
Let me pour water for Thy feet,
While the crowd goes by in the Street.

Why wouldst Thou dream of spear or sword,
Or of the ingrate rabble, Lord?
There is no sound save the song of a bird.

Let us sit down and talk at ease
About Thy Father's business.
(What shouts were those borne on the breeze?)

Nay, Lord, it cannot be for Thee
They raise the tallest cross of the three
On yon dark Mount of Calvary!

So soon, so soon, the hour's flown!
The glory's dying: Thou art gone
Out on Thy lonely way, alone.

The Wall Between
The wall between is grown so thin
That whoso peers may see
A flutter of rose, a living green
Like new leaves on a tree.

The wall's now gotten many a chink
Where whoso leans may hear
The feet of them who pass to drink
All at a well clear.

The people go, the people flow
T'other side o' the wall
With silken rustle and laughter low
As to a festival.

Come mother and wife and piteous bride,
The wall's nigh broken through;
And there be some the other side
That peep and pry for you.

So thin has grown, like a precious stone,
The wall no eye might pass,
You may have vision of your own
As through a crystal glass.

And if that sight should you delight
Your tears will all be dried,
For souls so bright that walk in white
Dear bliss on the other side.

New Heaven

Paradise now has many a Knight,
Many a lordkin, many lords,
Glimmer of armor, dinted and bright,
The young Knights have put on new swords.

Some have barely down on the lip,
Smiling yet from the new-won spurs,
Their wounds are rubies, glowing and deep,
Their scars amethyst-glorious scars.

Michael's army hath many new men,
Gravest Knights that may sit in stall
Kings and Captains, a shining train,
But the little young Knights are dearest of all.

Paradise now is the soldiers land
Their own country its shining sod,
Comrades all in a merry band;
And the young Knights' Laughter pleaseth God.

The Predestined

Dear, we might have known you were
To die young and were we blind
To the light or face and hair?
Dear, so simple and so kind.

You were clean as your own sword
And as straight too and steel true.
In the Army of the Lord
What promotion waits for you!

I can see you where you stand,
Knightly soul, so clean, so brave.
With a new sword in your hand
Where the lilied banners wave.

Flower of simple chivalry,
Marked for honour and for grace;
It was very plain to see
The clear shining of your face.

You are gone now: it's turned cold:
Very good you were and dear.
Wear the looks you wore of old
When we meet, some other year.

To One In Grief
Simon the Cyrenean bore
The Cross of Christ up Calvary Hill.
Blessed be Simon's lot before
Honour and ease and world's good-will
You, you would choose his lot above
All gifts and glories, yea, all love!

Now when for your two glorious men
Your heart is broken, and your joy
On earth shall not be built again,
Oh, what a lover, what a boy!
Dear heart, look up! Who helps you on
The way that you must walk alone?

For when the Cross that you must bear
Galls your poor shoulders till they bleed,
And when the thorns are on your hair,
And Love-lies-bleeding: then indeed
One will come stepping light and take
The tears the burden, the heart-break.

Happy is she who to Thine ears
Pours all her lamentations! Yea,
When Thou dost wipe away her tears

And healing words of comfort say.
Thou makest Thy Cross both sweet and light
For souls like hers that walk in white.

Printed in Great Britain
by Amazon

38726816R00032